Photograp[hs by]
Robert Smith
Michael White

Your First
PUPPY

CONTENTS

PO7 6AR
ENGLAND

Kingdom Books is an imprint of T.F.H. Publications
Printed in England.

INTRODUCTION

The dog: man's best friend. How many children, and adults too, dream of owning a small, cute and playful puppy that will grow up to be a big, handsome dog, protector of its owner and faithful companion? Many people have this vision about owning a dog. It is a scenario that can come true - but only with a great deal of hard work and careful consideration from the dog's owner.

A puppy does not become house-trained automatically, nor will it ever learn how to behave if it is not trained properly. An untrained dog can be a real nuisance and a danger. Have you enough time to care for a puppy? A puppy will not need many walks while it is very young, but when it grows up it will need regular walks, every day, no matter what the weather is like. Are you away from home during the greater part of the day? If so, I am afraid a dog is not the pet for you. Dogs are pack animals, and they need company. Buying two puppies instead of one is no substitute for human companionship. Some people claim that they manage to work full time yet

A small, cute, playful puppy - but it will need looking after for many years to come.

still own a dog, as they walk the dog first thing in the morning and as soon as they arrive home in the evening, but what sort of a life is that for a dog? It is quite reasonable to leave an adult dog on its own for four to five hours a day, but a young puppy can only be left for short periods at a time. If you leave your dog outside in a kennel, even if it has a big run, there is the risk of a barking dog annoying your neighbours. If you are out all day, you will either have to forget your dream about owning a dog, or ask around to see if you can find somebody willing to exercise your dog for an hour or so while you are away.

Never give in to children's pleas for a puppy of their own, believing their promises that they will walk and care for it. The novelty will wear off; no young child should be expected to have sole care of a dog. The ultimate responsibility lies with the adult. Where you live shouldn't really matter, as there are so many dog breeds to choose from, and there certainly are dogs small enough to live happily in a flat with no garden. But bear in mind that pets are banned from many flats in this country, and house-training will be much more difficult without a garden. You will also have to walk the dog at least four times a day if it has no access to a garden.

Finally, can you afford to own a dog? Buying a puppy may not be a great expense, especially if you have decided on a mongrel, but the cost of feeding your puppy, veterinary treatment such as annual vaccinations, and equipment such as collars, leads and dog beds will soon mount up. If you are still sure that you will make a good dog owner, and can offer everything that a puppy and adult dog will need, then you are to be congratulated. You are about to acquire a special friend!

SELECTION

Having decided that a puppy is the pet for you, the time has come for the all-important decision: which breed should you acquire? There are literally hundreds of dog breeds, so there is bound to be one to suit you and your lifestyle. Take care not to base your choice on looks alone. Different breeds have different temperaments and different behaviour patterns, and what suits one person may not suit another. Read books about dog breeds and visit dog shows. Ask people you see exercising their dogs in your local park; most dog owners will only be too pleased to discuss their dog's virtues. You can also contact local dog clubs for advice (The Kennel Club can supply you with details).

The bulldog may not come first in a beauty competition but can still be the right dog for you.

Don't rush your decision, but take plenty of time, making sure that everyone in your family agrees on the choice of breed. If you make the wrong decision, you will all suffer, people and pets alike. I once acquired a dog of a breed very different from the one that I usually keep, thinking that I knew what this breed was like, and that it would fit nicely into my home. A year later I had come to realise that my choice had been utterly wrong. The dog was far too lively to fit in with my family and it didn't get on with our cats.

A dog does not have to be a pedigree to make a lovely pet.

As I was unable to give the dog as much exercise as this particular breed needs, I ended up with a bored dog who took her frustration out on my kitchen, literally chewing it to pieces. Eventually she had to go to a more suitable family. The next time I decided to buy a puppy of a breed that I had not owned before, I read every single book on the breed that I could find, spoke to dog breeders and dog trainers, and did not make my final choice until I was one hundred per cent sure that this breed would be right for my family.

Of course, many people will opt for a crossbreed or mongrel rather than a pedigree dog. Mongrels can make fantastic pets, and there is nothing at all that says that a dog is better simply because it is pure-bred and has a pedigree. However, neither is it true that mongrels are healthier than pedigree dogs and are therefore a better choice. Many breeds do suffer from hereditary diseases, but any caring breeder will have been careful to breed only from dogs and bitches that are free from these. As a prospective buyer, you have every right to ask the breeder to show you certificates relating to screening for hereditary eye diseases and hip dysplasia. Again, by reading up on your chosen breed before the purchase, you will know what to look out for. And as for mongrels being healthier, how many mongrels are being screened for problems such as hip dysplasia? Not many. Therefore, the truth could be that mongrels suffer from just as many hereditary problems as pedigrees. General health problems are often seen in mongrels as well as pedigrees, so concern for your puppy's health need not be a deciding factor in your choice of pedigree or mongrel. Finally, unless you opt for an adult dog rather than a puppy, it can be difficult to tell how big a mongrel puppy will grow and what temperament it will have. If you want a dog of a particular size and

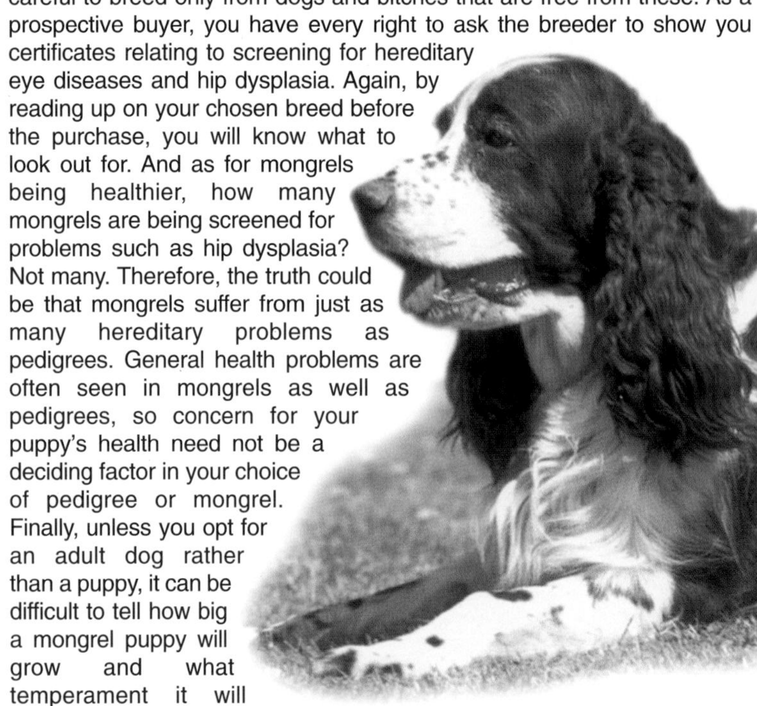

The Spaniel is a gundog, but makes an excellent family pet.

temperament you are probably better off buying a pedigree, as then you will have some idea what it will be like as an adult. However, if you have no special criteria, a mongrel or cross-breed could work out just as well.

In Britain, pedigree dogs are divided into six different breed groups. The dogs within one group are often similar to one another in several ways, including temperament. The breed groups are as follows:

Gundogs: This group includes the very popular Labrador and Golden Retriever, as well as other Retriever breeds such as the Flatcoated Retriever. It includes all Setter breeds (Irish, Irish Red and White, English and Gordon), English and German Pointers, and Spaniels (including Cocker, Clumber, Springer and Field). Gundogs were originally bred as shooting companions. These days, most gundogs are family pets, even if many do still work in their original capacity too. Setter and Retriever breeds make excellent family pets, but they do need a great deal of exercise and training. Spaniels tend to be livelier than other gundogs.

Hounds: This group includes hounds as different as the Afghan, the Bloodhound, the Beagle, the Dachshund (in several different coat and size varieties), the Greyhound and the Whippet, to name but a few. Hounds were all originally hunting and tracking dogs, and several, such as the Greyhound and Whippet, are used in racing today. Hounds can make good family pets, but many will not get on with other animals, such as cats, and they may need a lot of training.

Terriers: The Terrier group includes all Terriers with the exception of those like the Yorkshire Terrier that are small enough to be classified as Toy breeds. Popular Terriers include the West Highland White Terrier ('Westie'), the Scottish Terrier ('Scottie'), the Border Terrier, the Staffordshire Bull Terrier, the Fox Terrier (Wire and Smooth), and the Airedale Terrier. Terriers were originally used as hunting dogs, often hunting rabbits and other prey underground in burrows. The 'terrier instinct' is still present in most Terrier breeds, producing tough, fearless dogs that will need firm training to keep them in line, and that may be best kept in a house where there are no smaller pets. Properly trained, a Terrier will make a marvellous companion, and even the smallest ones have great stamina that will enable them to go for long walks in any weather.

Toy dogs: These are the smallest breeds whose only function is to be companion dogs. The Toy group includes the popular Yorkshire Terrier (who remains a Terrier in temperament!), the happy and friendly Cavalier King Charles Spaniel, the tiny Chihuahua who comes with either a long or smooth coat, the Papillon (known as the Butterfly dog because of its ears),

A Bedlington Terrier and her pup. When choosing a pup, always try to see him with his mothe

Terriers need firm training to keep them in line, as they are tough little dogs with plenty of stamina!

the Pekingese and the Pug, to name a few. Breeds in the Toy group differ vastly, so no generalisations can be made about their behaviour and temperament.

Utility dogs: Again, the main function of these breeds nowadays is as pet dogs, although some may originally have had a more specific purpose. The Utility group includes many breeds, such as the Dalmatian, all varieties of Poodle, the English and French Bulldog, the Miniature and Standard Schnauzer, and the Shih Tzu. They differ considerably in temperament, but most make very good family pets.

Working dogs: These are exactly what they sound like: dogs bred to do a specific job, such as guarding sheep. The Working group is very big, including popular breeds such as the German Shepherd Dog (Alsatian), the Border Collie, the Rough and Smooth Collies, the Rottweiler, the Dobermann, the Great Dane, the Newfoundland, the Saint Bernard, the Siberian Husky and the Welsh Corgi. Many working breeds need a considerable amount of exercise and training in order to live happy lives. They are demanding dogs and should not be chosen unless you have plenty of time to devote to them. A properly trained dog of a Working breed is a marvellous companion.

WHERE TO OBTAIN YOUR PUPPY

Having decided what you want, you must decide where to obtain your puppy. The only two really reliable sources are a **reputable breeder** (The Kennel Club can supply you both with a list of breeders that have puppies available and a list of breed clubs that can recommend breeders) or a **Rescue Centre** such as the RSPCA or the National Canine Defence League. In the United Kingdom it is unusual for puppies to be sold in pet shops, although in some countries there are specialist outlets that sell them. A good breeder will be able to show you the mother of the puppies. Only buy a puppy from somebody who appears to care for his or her dogs and will not sell a puppy before being satisfied that **you** will be a good dog owner. He or she will ask many questions about your home and lifestyle, which should not be seen as prying but as a sign of the breeder's concern for the pups. Rescue Centre staff will do this, too.

SELECTING YOUR PUPPY

Ideally, the puppy you select should be about eight weeks old. If obtained at this age, the puppy will be properly weaned and ready to leave home, but still young enough to settle easily into a new home. Training will be much easier when you start with a young pup rather than an older one.

Having said that, it may work out perfectly well to buy a slightly older puppy, provided that he has had some sort of socialisation and is used to people and everyday life. Breeders often 'run on' puppies until they are about six months old before they finally decide which to keep back for showing and which to sell. Such a puppy can be a very good buy, but **not** if it has been kept permanently in a kennel with few experiences of ordinary life.

Make sure you have everything your puppy will need before you bring him home. These pups have their own, custom-made dog bed.

If you are lucky enough to be able to choose one puppy out of an entire litter, take care when making your choice. It always used to be said that puppy buyers should reject the quiet, withdrawn puppy, opting rather for the bold one that immediately bounds towards them. However, this is not necessarily true. Consider what sort of person you are, and try to match the puppy to **your** personality. Ask the breeder for help if you are not sure, as he or she will probably know the puppies and their personalities. It is no good selecting the boldest puppy if you are a quiet, gentle sort of person, as this may well be the puppy that needs a firm hand. Likewise, if you are very outgoing with a loud voice and given to sudden movements, selecting the quiet puppy may be a disaster. For most people, the 'middle of the road' puppy is probably the best choice; the one that neither is the first nor the last to come up to you to say 'hello'.

Check that the puppy you have selected appears to be healthy. It should be alert when awake and react when spoken to.The eyes should be bright and clear, the nose clean. Puppies usually have a clear discharge from their nostrils, but this should be like water, not thick or coloured.The tail area should look clean, and the ears should be free of discharge.The skin should be pale and soft without any red spots. Puppies love to get dirty, so do not be put off if the puppy's fur is a bit dirty; usually all it means is that the puppy has had great fun playing outdoors with its litter-mates.

DOG OR BITCH?

Which sex is very much a matter of personal choice. Some people claim that bitches make better pets; others prefer dogs. Each dog is an individual, and behaviour varies considerably with breeds, but as a general rule it can be said that bitches are less lively than dogs, but more prone to sulk. A bitch may be easier to call in when off the lead than a dog, and she will often pull less on the lead. At the same time, a dog may be more playful than a bitch. The choice really is yours.

A word on neutering here: any unneutered bitch will come into season twice a year, usually every six months. When she does, she will have a bloody discharge for around three weeks, and will be receptive to mating for part of this time. During all the time she will be the object of much interest to male dogs. Being in season may also make the bitch more sulky than usual. When she is in season, she must be kept on a lead at all times, or she will soon be mated. You do not want to bring unplanned puppies into the world; there are too many of them already.

Most vets recommend that bitches not intended for breeding be neutered (spayed). This is a good permanent solution to the hassle of seasons, but it is by no means the only solution. A properly supervised bitch who, when in season, is kept on a lead and not allowed to wander is no more likely to produce unwanted puppies than is a spayed bitch. The spaying of bitches, although it is carried out routinely, is a major operation in which the bitch's womb is removed. In some breeds, neutering will alter coat texture. Similarly, a properly supervised dog who does not roam the streets will not give rise to unwanted puppies.The spaying of bitches and castration of dogs doesn't have to be done and, if you want to show your dog, is better not done. Neutered dogs and bitches do not necessarily make better pets or have better temperaments. Such factors depend mainly on inherited characteristics and training. Use your own common sense when deciding whether or not to neuter.

BRINGING YOUR NEW PUPPY HOME

When you travel home with your new puppy, it should sit on your lap to feel secure. Talk to it gently, and the chances are that it will soon fall asleep. Ask the breeder not to feed the puppy for a few hours before you are due to collect it, just in case it gets car sick. Many puppies do, but this phase often passes as the puppy grows older.

Before collecting your puppy you should set up a quiet corner in your home where it can rest in peace and quiet and feel secure. Its bed could be a specially bought dog bed, a blanket inside an old cardboard box (puppies do tend to chew, so you may be better off not buying an expensive bed until he is older), or a dog pen (cage) with a blanket in. A bowl of water should be available, and preferably some toys to chew. Newspapers should be spread on the floor for the puppy to do its business on, but not too close to its sleeping quarters, as puppies do not like messing close to where they sleep. It is probably best if the

This Golden Retriever pup will need plenty of exercise as he gets older.

puppy is confined to one room to start with. To stop it from entering other rooms, you can place a child-gate across the doorway. If the puppy is such a small one that it will simply walk through the bars of the gate, tie wire netting across them.

Let the puppy explore its new home. Talk to it and reassure it that everything is all right, using its name. Do not let children disturb it too much, as young puppies need a lot of sleep. At night, you will probably want your puppy to sleep in its own bed. Naturally, it will feel rather lonely having left its mother and litter-mates, so it may cry. Try not to give in to this and bring the puppy into your bedroom. If you give in on the first night you will never get it to sleep alone. If your puppy cries, speak to it through the closed door, telling it gently but firmly to be quiet and go to sleep. Avoid going into the room to see your puppy as this will only teach it that crying will make its owner appear. An old tried and tested trick is to put a hot water bottle and a ticking clock under the blanket in the puppy's bed. This will remind the puppy of its mother; the water bottle will imitate the body warmth of the bitch, and the ticking clock her heart beat.

If your puppy is eight weeks or more and has not yet received any vaccinations you should take it along to the vet as soon as possible to have this done. Your vet will also give your puppy a check-up to make sure that it is healthy and in good condition. You should not take your puppy out for walks until its vaccination programme has been completed. Most vets will advise exercise only in your own garden. However, as vaccinations are unlikely to be completed before the puppy is about four months old, your puppy will lose out on important early socialisation such as seeing people and traffic on the streets. If you are unlucky you could end up with a dog that is frightened of cars, people and new situations. A bold puppy who regularly sees many people at home may do well even if kept in until the vaccinations are completed, but a shy pup in a quiet home may need to get out and about earlier. Use your common sense in this respect, and talk to the puppy's breeder and veterinary surgeon for advice.

FEEDING

Feeding puppies can be a complex and bewildering subject. Ask the breeder or the rescue centre that sold you your puppy what diet he or she recommends. Your puppy will probably do best on the diet it is used to, as the breeder will no doubt have many years' experience of feeding puppies. It is very important to find out exactly what your puppy needs. Different breeds have different requirements and a small Terrier, for example, **cannot** be fed in a similar way to a Saint Bernard. It is not simply a question of how much food the puppy should have: the amounts of protein, calcium and vitamins are also important. So always ask the breeder. If your puppy did not come from a reputable breeder, ask your vet.

These curly-coated retriever pups are enjoying one of their four meals a day.

There are three main ways of feeding puppies and dogs. The traditional way is to feed canned meat together with biscuit-meal, often called a 'mixer'. These days complete dry foods are becoming more and more popular, as these need nothing added to them except water. Some people prefer a more natural diet, consisting of meat, vegetables, bread, and cereal. With such a diet, vitamins and calcium must be added at the correct dosage for your particular puppy. Again, ask for advice.

Puppies up to four or five months should receive four meals a day. One of these is often a milk meal, preferably powdered milk manufactured especially for dogs. At four to five months your puppy should receive three meals. From six to eight months of age (depending on breed, small breeds maturing much earlier than large ones) two meals will be sufficient. This is also better for an adult dog. (A dog is classified as adult once twelve months old.) Some people give just one meal a day, but most dogs prefer two, as it

Puppies should not leave their mother or litter-mates before the age of eight weeks.

is kinder to their stomachs. Certain breeds, (especially the giant ones) are prone to a condition known as gastric torsion, and for these breeds it is important to feed smaller meals, as one large meal can be too much for the dog. The tendons holding the stomach in place snap, turning the stomach over inside the dog. This condition is fatal if not treated surgically at once.

TREATS

Avoid giving your puppy treats in between meals, as he may put on too much weight or refuse to eat his main meals. If you want to give treats of any kind, give them as a reward when training your puppy. Choose healthy treats manufactured for dogs and, when treats have been given, slightly reduce the amount of the proper meal. For teeth exercise, there are many chews to choose from. Hard natural bones are not good and some bones, such as chicken, can splinter dangerously. A safe product like Nylabone Puppybone, obtainable from your pet shop, is best.

This puppy is alert and interested - a sign of his good health.

EQUIPMENT

There is a bewildering array of dog products available nowadays, from simple leather collars to special doggy umbrellas to attach to your dog's lead, and everything in between. Much is unnecessary, most is useful, and some items are vital. These are the items which you will certainly need:

Collar: For a puppy, this should be a soft collar made of fabric or leather. By law, a disc bearing your address and telephone number must be attached. For adult dogs, your choice of collar should depend on the size of your dog and how it behaves on the lead. A small, well-behaved dog can have a soft leather collar throughout its life. A larger dog that may sometimes pull on the lead is better off with a so-called 'half choke' collar. This is a collar that is partly leather or fabric, partly chain. When the dog pulls, the chain tightens, but not completely: only to a set degree. This is far kinder than the choke chain, which these days must be seen as an outdated method of stopping your dog from pulling on the lead. A choke chain can seriously damage your dog's throat and neck if used incorrectly. Excellent headcollars are available for strong dogs that pull a lot on the lead. These stop the dog from pulling without causing any discomfort.

Lead: The best type of lead is the leather lead. It may cost a lot more than other leads, but it should last for the entire lifespan of your dog, and probably for your next dog as well. Leather leads are soft and comfortable to hold, yet strong. A fabric lead can do very well if your dog does not pull on its lead. If it does, you may get friction burns on your hands. Leads that consist mainly of chain should not be used as they are uncomfortable and impractical for both dog and owner. No dog is strong enough to break a good quality leather or fabric lead of suitable size by pulling on it.

Leads are available in different lengths and widths. The bigger the dog, the wider the lead should be. For a small dog, the lead can be shorter than for a big one. So-called extending leads, which roll out of a plastic case, can be very useful, especially for exercising a bitch in season, or for training. However, care should be taken. Accidents have happened where the lead has not been properly locked, and dogs have run out into the road. Rope leads, made entirely out of rope or nylon, can be very useful for the dog that does not pull much, and also at dog shows. The lead forms a loop, thus becoming collar and lead in one. The collar will then be of the choke type, but as it is not made of chain it is kinder to the dog. This type, however, should only be used on fairly large dogs, such as Labradors.

Food and water bowls: Any dog will need access to water at all times as well as a bowl for its meals. The best type of food and water bowl is made of lightweight metal and available in many different sizes, as it is unbreakable and easy to keep clean. If your dog tends to knock a lightweight bowl over or to carry it around (Retriever breeds often do this) an earthenware bowl would be a good choice.

Bed: A dog should have its own bed to retreat to when it wants peace and quiet. Dogs should not sleep in their owners' beds, because this will confuse the pecking order. As the owner, you are top dog in the pack, and therefore the underdog will not be allowed into your den! As mentioned earlier, the best bed for a puppy is a simple cardboard box with a blanket in it. A more elaborate bed will probably get chewed. Once adult, the dog can graduate to a proper bed. There are many designs, but make sure that you choose one that is big enough for your dog to lay down comfortably and is easy to keep clean.

Brushes and combs: All dogs need grooming; how much and how often will depend on the type of coat. This will also decide what type of comb and brush you will need.Your puppy's breeder and the staff in your local pet shop can advise you about this.

Nail clippers: All dogs need to have their nails trimmed regularly so that these do not grow too long. Many kinds of nailclipper are available in pet shops.

These pups are enjoying playing with their Nylabone Plaque Attacker Dental Floss, and it's good for their teeth, too!

Toys: All dogs like toys to play with. Choose toys that are safe for the dog, neither soft enough to be chewed to pieces that can then be swallowed nor small enough to be swallowed whole. The staff in your pet shop will be able to show you the Nylabone range of products, which includes a wide variety of safe and beneficial chewing articles.

At the end of the day, a chap likes to find a comfortable place to lie down...

Your pup needs lots of love and attention so that it can grow strong and healthy.

GENERAL CARE

Your dog's general care will include grooming. As has already been indicated, the extent and frequency will depend on the type of coat. For example, a Yorkshire Terrier will need daily combing, whereas a Boxer will just need the occasional brushing. Many breeds, such as Poodles, Spaniels and most Terriers, will need regular professional grooming. Poodles will need to be clipped every six weeks, with regular brushings between, to look their best. Rough coated terriers will need to be hand-stripped twice a year, a process that involves the removal of old, dead fur by hand. These procedures are not easy to learn, and most people will take their dog to a grooming parlour. Ask your dog's breeder for advice on grooming.

Nails will need trimming when they start to grow too long, usually every other month. You can learn to do this yourself but, if you are at all unsure, ask your vet or dog groomer to show you how. Your dog's ears will need to be kept clean. In the case of short-coated dogs, this only entails ensuring that the ears look and smell clean. Other breeds, especially those like Poodles that have quantities of fur inside their ears, will need to have the excess fur plucked out regularly to prevent the ear canals from becoming too warm and air-tight, as this can cause problems.

Most dogs will need the occasional bath: how often will depend on coat type and how dirty your dog gets. Always stand your dog on a rubber mat inside the bath. Use lukewarm water and a shampoo intended for dogs.Take care not to get water or shampoo into the dog's eyes or ears, and to rinse out all of the shampoo. Towel dry vigorously afterwards.

Your dog's teeth will need attention. Sooner or later, all dogs will start to develop tartar, a brown, hard matter on the teeth. If it is not removed, gum disease and tooth loss will result. Small breeds are especially prone to tartar. You can help prevent tartar by brushing your dog's teeth regularly, using a soft toothbrush and special dog toothpaste available from pet shops. Alternatively, obtain a dentist's tooth scraper and gently scrape any tartar off your dog's teeth as soon as it appears. All dogs can be trained to behave well enough for you to do this, and you will save a fortune in vet's bills. If your dog suffers badly from tartar, a vet will have to descale its teeth.

TRAINING

All dogs need to be trained to a certain degree so that they will become acceptable members of society. Even the smallest Yorkshire Terrier needs to be properly trained. Training can start as soon as you bring your puppy home, as dogs learn most easily as young puppies. Some breeds are easier to train than others, but **all** are trainable. You may not want to take part in the obedience championships at Crufts, but you will want a well-behaved dog that will be a pleasure to live with and won't be a nuisance or danger to anyone.

The basic training that all dogs should receive is described below. For further advice, read a book on the subject or contact your local dog training club.

House-training: The first lesson a puppy needs to learn is to be clean in the house. This is achieved by vigilance and praise, **not** by punishment. Watch your puppy carefully. Every time it shows signs of needing to relieve itself (such as starting to circle) take it outside. Take your pup outside every time it wakes up from a nap, after a game, and after each meal, as these are the times when it is most likely to need to do its business. Once your puppy performs outside, give it lots of praise. If you use a command such as 'busy dog' every time your dog performs where it is meant to, you may even be able to teach it to 'go' on command. If your dog has an accident indoors, **don't** scold: this will only confuse it and make matters worse. Put down newspapers near the door for the puppy to use if you can't get him outside in time. Carried out properly, house-training can be achieved in about a week, but bear in mind that young puppies have very small bladders and so will be physically incapable of holding on for too long a time, such as overnight.

Walking on a lead: All puppies will object at first to wearing a collar and lead, so do not rush him. Start by making your pup wear the collar and lead indoors or in the garden. Don't pull on the lead, but gently call your puppy and encourage it to follow you. Once it has got used to the idea of a lead, you can pull it gently in the right direction. Use plenty of praise and possibly treats as well. If trained correctly, your dog should never start to pull on the lead.

Coming when called: Take every opportunity you get to call your puppy to you. Your puppy should learn to associate you with fun and food. Call its name and 'come' (such as 'Rufus, come!') at feeding time, when you want to play with it, or just to give it a cuddle. Do not make the mistake of only calling your dog when you want to put it on the lead, as it will then soon learn that being called will mean a loss of freedom, so will **not** come. When

It is a good idea to start training your pup from an early age so that he becomes an acceptable member of society.

walking your puppy off the lead, call it while running away from it. This will soon encourage it to come to you, as no puppy likes to be left on its own. If recall is trained from an early enough age, it need never be a problem.

Teaching your puppy to sit: Hold a treat in one hand and let the puppy see this. Raise your hand with the treat above the puppy's head so that it looks up. At the same time, say 'sit' and gently press down on its bottom with your other hand. When it sits, give your puppy the treat. If you use this method it should only take you a day at the most to teach your puppy to sit.

Teaching your puppy to lie down: First get your puppy to sit. Then take a treat in one hand and hold it in front of your puppy's nose. Put your hand down on the floor and slowly pull the treat away from the puppy. Give the command 'down' at the same time. Most puppies will lay down automatically, but if it does not you can help by sliding your other arm under its front legs, gently pulling them down.

Teaching your puppy to stay: Have your puppy in a sitting position, with a lead attached to its collar. Say 'stay' and move away a very small distance, while holding the lead. If the dog stays, praise it and give a treat. If it gets up, try again. You may have to put a hand gently on its collar to start with. Once it has the idea, you can move further away gradually. Don't let your dog get up until you have walked back to it. This exercise can be a life-saver. For instance, if your puppy is running off towards a road with heavy traffic, call 'sit!' and 'stay!' and, if trained correctly, your dog will do just this.

General good behaviour: All dogs should be taught the word 'no', which will come in handy many a time. You can train this by putting a treat on the floor, and then walking past it with your dog on a lead. When your dog tries to take the treat, say 'no' and pull its head away. After a few times, use the opposite command 'okay' (or something similar) and let the dog have the treat. The word 'no' can be used for any situation.

A basketful of Boxers!

Even if you have bought a well-bred puppy whose parents have been screened for all possible hereditary diseases, it is probable that your dog will contract one kind of illness or another during its life. If you are ever unsure about your dog's health, see a veterinary surgeon.

Vaccinations: All puppies should be vaccinated against distemper, hepatitis, leptospirosis and parvovirus. Annual booster injections will then be necessary. These diseases are virtually incurable and nearly always fatal, as well as being very contagious, so annual boosters are a 'must'. It is also possible to vaccinate against kennel cough, a less serious disease. Ask your vet for details.

Ear problems: Not many dogs will go through life without ever contracting any sort of ear problem. Signs of ear trouble include the dog scratching its ears, rubbing its ears on your carpet, and producing a discharge that can vary in colour but is usually smelly. See a vet, who will give you drops to treat the condition, and show you how to clean the ears. Normally, a dog's ears do not need cleaning.

Eye problems: These often occur if the dog has been sitting in a draught or sticking its head out of the car window when the car is in motion. A yellow or green discharge can be seen from the eye, and the eye and eyelids may be red. See a vet who will prescribe drops or ointment.

Skin problems: These are common and can take many forms. Hair loss and reddening of the skin or actual sores anywhere on the body can have many causes. Some dogs are allergic to flea bites, so fleas should always be eliminated by means of a good quality flea spray or another flea product. Ask your vet or pet shop for advice. Other dogs can have food allergies. For any type of skin problem, see your vet, who will try to establish the cause and find the correct treatment.

Worms: It is very important to worm your dog regularly, approximately four times a year. All dogs need worming against roundworm *(Toxocara canis)* and, if they have been flea-infested, they will probably need worming against tapeworm as well. The *Toxocara canis* worm has been the subject of much hysteria in the media. If unwormed, the dog may pass worm eggs through its faeces, which will then develop into larvae if left on the ground for a couple of weeks. If accidentally ingested these larvae can cause the disease Toxocariasis in humans, which is often said to cause blindness in children. However, the disease is rare, and no human has ever been totally blinded by it. Any dog owner should worm his or her dog regularly and, of course, always pick up after the dog when out walking it. If this is done, no

A glossy coat, bright eyes and alert expression show that this Retriever pup is in the pink of conditio

This bold pup may need firm training so that he does not come to dominate his owner.

worm eggs in the dog's faeces get a chance to develop into larvae, and nobody wants to walk in dog mess, do they? Ask your vet for advice on the best worming preparations.

Impacted anal glands: The anal glands are two sacs situated either side of the dog's anus. A liquid is secreted from these when the dog passes a motion. Quite frequently, these sacs become blocked, and will start to cause the dog discomfort. A common sign of this is the dog dragging its bottom along the ground. A vet can empty these glands easily and show you how to do it yourself.

Longevity: A dog's natural lifespan depends on the breed. As a general rule, small breeds live longer than large ones. A Toy Poodle may live for 15 years or more, a Golden Retriever for 12 to 13 years, a Great Dane for only 8 to 10 years.

FURTHER INFORMATION:

Further information, particularly about your nearest breed club for your chosen breed or obedience and other dog activity clubs in your area, can be obtained from The Kennel Club at the following address:

The Kennel Club
1 Clarges Street, Piccadilly, London, W1Y 8AB, ENGLAND
Tel: 0171 493 6651

These addresses could also be useful:

National Canine Defence League (NCDL)
17 Wakley Street, London EC1V 7LT
Tel: 0171 837 0006

Royal Society for the Prevention of Cruelty to Animals (RSPCA)
Causeway, Horsham, West Sussex RH12 1HG
Tel: 01403 264181

People's Dispensary for Sick Animals (PDSA)
Whitechapel Way, Priorslee, Telford, Salop TF2 9PQ
Tel: 01952 290999

BIBLIOGRAPHY

ATLAS OF DOG BREEDS:
Bonnie Wilcox and Chris Walkowicz
H-1091
ISBN 0 79381 284 4
The ultimate dog breed identification guide, this book traces the history of every recognised dog breed.
Hardcover: 24cm x 32cm, 912 pages, over 1100 full-colour photos.

MINI-ATLAS OF DOG BREEDS
Andrew de Prisco and James B Johnson
H-1106
ISBN 0 86622 091 7
This up-to-date dog identification handbook gives descriptions and colour photographs of more than 400 breeds of dog around the world, some of which have never before been illustrated.The text is concise, informative and enjoyable.
Hardcover: 14.5cm x 22cm, 573 pages, over 500 colour photos.

LOVE ME, LOVE MY DOG: complete dog ownership manual
Barrie Curruthers, MD and Keith Bing, MBIPDT
TS-212
ISBN 0 79380 088 9
A user-friendly primer, written by experts, to guide prospective dog owners on such topics as selection, training, health care, housing and the legal aspects of dog ownership.
Hardcover: 18cm x 26cm, 254 pages, illustrated in full colour throughout.

OWNER'S GUIDE TO DOG HEALTH CARE:
Lowell Ackerman, DVM
TS-214
ISBN 0 79380 183 4
This book, written for the dog-owning layman by an internationally respected veterinary surgeon, provides readers with current, accurate information about new procedures and technological advances in all areas of canine care.
Hardcover: 18cm x 26cm, 432 pages, illustrated with hundreds of colour photos and drawings.

EVERYBODY CAN TRAIN THEIR OWN DOG: the essentials of dog training
Angela White
TW-113
ISBN 0 86622 524 2
Invaluable to all dog owners, this guide offers in layman's terms the key to successful dog training. All teaching methods are based on motivation and kindness which bring out and mould the dog's natural ability and instinct.
Hardcover: 13cm x 18.5cm, 255 pages, colour photos throughout.

BECOMING YOUR DOG'S BEST FRIEND: how to earn your dog's love
Martin J Becker, DVM
TS-220
ISBN 0 79380 087 0
An extremely readable book on practical dog care, with emphasis on the delights and responsibilities of dog ownership.
Softcover: 17.5cm x 21.5cm, 64 pages, illustrated in full colour throughout.